Earth Movement

by Carol Talley

PEARSON

Scott
Foresman

Editorial Offices: Glenview, Illinois • Parsippany, New Jersey • New York, New York
Sales Offices: Needham, Massachusetts • Duluth, Georgia • Glenview, Illinois
Coppell, Texas • Ontario, California • Mesa, Arizona

ISBN: 0-328-13366-3

It is the day you have been waiting for, the day of the canoe trip. The weather is going to be perfect. Last night you heard the weather forecaster on the radio say there would be clear skies and plenty of sunshine. But now the sky is getting dark. The air is getting cooler. Raindrops are starting to fall.

It looks like the weather prediction was wrong again!

Predicting weather is not easy. After all, nobody can really tell the future. Predictions are smart guesses about what might happen. They are built on things we have learned and on our knowledge about how things work.

As difficult as it is to predict the weather, scientists are discovering that it is even more difficult to predict where and when volcanic eruptions and earthquakes will happen. In fact, sometimes it seems almost impossible! Still, scientists keep working hard to learn more. If scientists can discover warning signs that a volcanic eruption or an earthquake is about to happen, they can help protect our homes and save our lives.

When will the volcano blow?

Volcanoes are erupting all the time. Some scientists estimate that about ten of Earth's fifteen hundred volcanoes erupt every day! **Volcanologists** have found many written references to volcanic eruptions. Since the start of recorded history people have written about at least five hundred different volcanic eruptions. Many more volcanoes erupted during **prehistoric** times, before records were kept.

Scientists know that some volcanoes that erupted in the past are still active. That means these volcanoes are likely to erupt again in the future.

A loaf of bread reduced to charcoal, from the first century A.D. eruption of Mount Vesuvius

Mount Vesuvius today. The crater is evidence of the mountain's eruptions.

On land, volcanoes can often be seen from miles away. When they erupt, some volcanoes create enormous amounts of noise and can damage everything around them.

A volcano may erupt and then sit quietly for hundreds or thousands of years. Or it could erupt twice or more in just a couple of years. To learn how to spot the warning signs of an eruption, scientists monitor many volcanoes. *Monitor* means to keep a record, like a journal, of all the changes that go on around a volcano, day after day, year after year.

Volcano Monitoring

In 1847 the first volcano **observatory** was created in Italy. The people who worked there monitored Vesuvius, the volcano that destroyed the city of Herculaneum in A.D. 79.

Modern volcano monitoring really began, however, when scientists built the Hawaiian Volcano Observatory on the rim of Kilauea. Kilauea is one of the world's most active volcanoes. This observatory also sits near the Mauna Loa volcano, which is almost as active as Kilauea. Scientists at this observatory have developed methods for monitoring volcanoes that are now used all over the world.

People watch smoke and ash rise from the crater of Mount Vesuvius during an eruption in the 1930s.

After many years of monitoring volcanoes, scientists are becoming very skilled at spotting the warning signs of an eruption. They have learned that before an eruption, three things usually happen.

By monitoring these events, scientists hope to predict when a volcano eruption is coming. Let's look more closely at how this is done.

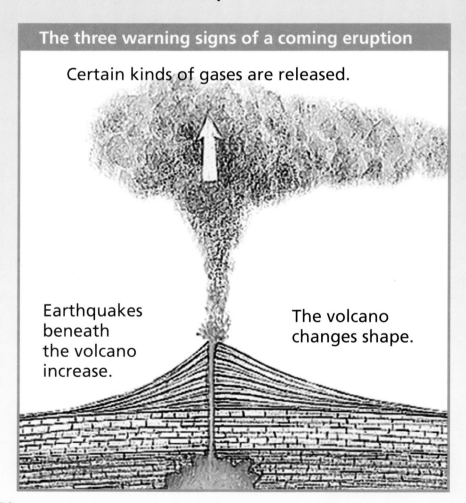

The three warning signs of a coming eruption

Certain kinds of gases are released.

Earthquakes beneath the volcano increase.

The volcano changes shape.

Bulges and Tilts

When hot **magma** rises up inside a volcano, the sides of the volcano may bulge, tilt, or crack. Volcanologists use special instruments that can measure and record these changes, even if the changes are very small.

A tiltmeter is an **instrument** that measures tiny changes in the slant of the ground. Tiltmeters have been used to monitor the shape of volcanoes for many years. Tiltmeters are rather simple when compared to modern equipment. But they are still very effective for predicting eruptions. In 1980 a tiltmeter helped scientists predict the eruption of Mount St. Helens in Washington State.

Today, instead of tiltmeters, volcanologists rely mostly on satellites and the Global Positioning System, or GPS, to measure volcanoes. You might have ridden in a car with a GPS system. GPS can be used to provide directions for drivers. It can also be used to monitor changes in a volcano's shape.

Shakes and Quakes

It is common for small earthquakes to occur beneath active volcanoes. Some volcanoes send out weak vibrations all the time. When magma and volcanic gases force their way up inside a volcano before an eruption, the earthquakes usually increase in strength and number.

Scientist inspecting seismometers

An important part of monitoring a volcano is to record the strength of these earthquakes and where they happen inside the volcano. To do this, volcanologists use seismometers. Seismometers are instruments that measure movements in the ground. Volcanologists sometimes set up a **network** of seismometers around a volcano.

Escaping Gases

As magma rises inside a volcano, gases escape from the top or from weak spots on the sides. Scientists constantly check to see what gases are released. They sometimes have to go high up on the volcano to collect gases for testing. While scientists are working on top of a volcano, they are exposed to many dangers, including poisonous **fumes** and the risk of a sudden eruption.

Sometimes it is possible to put instruments near the tops of volcanoes to collect and measure gases automatically. Other times volcanic gases can be measured from aboard an aircraft or from a satellite.

Kilauea Volcano, Hawaii

Progress Report

There are now five volcano observatories in the United States. Volcanoes are also being monitored in Italy, Japan, New Zealand, and Russia, as well as several other countries. Scientists are not able to predict the exact time and place of an eruption. Still, every year they learn more about the warning signs that are given off before an eruption.

Earthquakes seem to be even more difficult to predict than volcanic eruptions. Some scientists think it might be impossible for humans to ever have success in predicting earthquakes.

Predicting Unpredictable Earthquakes

The world has about eighteen major earthquakes each year. Earthquakes can happen anywhere. Most big earthquakes occur along the edges of the Pacific Ocean, where several of the huge plates that form Earth's crust meet. These plates are not like the ones you eat dinner from! Instead, they contain mile after mile of solid rock. When the plates rub together, they can cause earthquakes.

As with volcanic eruptions, scientists know a lot about where earthquakes are likely to happen. So far scientists are not able to predict when an actual earthquake is about to strike.

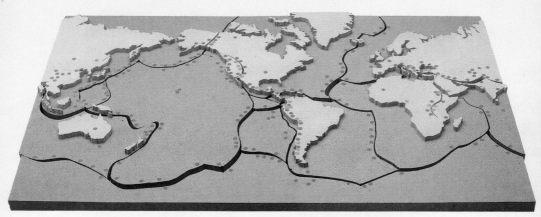

Earthquakes usually happen along the plate boundaries of Earth's surface.

A theodolite is used to detect changes in a volcano's shape.

For many years, earthquake scientists in the United States studied California's San Andreas **Fault,** which is formed by the North American and Pacific plates. The scientists studying the San Andreas Fault were hoping to discover the signals that would warn when future earthquakes were coming.

But earthquakes are not like volcanoes. They do not seem to give off warning signals. After many years of monitoring the San Andreas Fault, scientists now know more about this earthquake area than any other in the world. But they have not successfully predicted the exact time and place of a single earthquake.

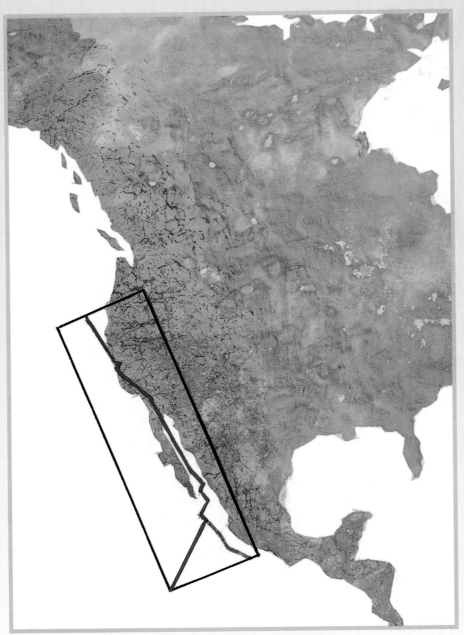

The San Andreas Fault, shown here in blue, runs
for hundreds of miles.

The Parkfield Earthquake Prediction Experiment

Since 1857, six strong earthquakes have struck the small town of Parkfield, California, located on the San Andreas Fault. When the next one strikes, scientists plan to be there! Since 1985, the United States Geological Survey, or USGS, has focused much of its earthquake monitoring on this one location.

Monitoring an earthquake zone is a lot like monitoring a volcano. Scientists at Parkfield look for three of the same warning signals that volcanologists monitor. They are watching for changes in the shape of the land and the release of certain gases. They also pay close attention to earthquakes!

So, you might ask, how can an earthquake serve as a warning that another earthquake is on the way? The reason is that small earthquakes, called foreshocks, sometimes come before the main earthquake, called the mainshock. There are seismometers in forty places near Parkfield to measure every small movement of the ground.

Scientists have also noticed that the level of water in wells may change before an earthquake. Wells are fed by groundwater. Groundwater rises up from the spaces and cracks in rocks deep in the ground. If there is extra pressure on these rocks, the groundwater might be pushed higher or deeper into the rocks. This can cause the water level in wells to go up or down. Scientists at Parkfield use special instruments that measure any changes in water level.

A geodimeter at the Parkfield Earthquake Experiment emits laser light while analyzing the San Andreas Fault in California.

Still Waiting

In the 1980s, after studying the history of earthquakes near Parkfield, scientists predicted that a damaging earthquake would hit the town between 1988 and 1992. Fortunately for Parkfield, the prediction never came true. Still, earthquake scientists in California continue to monitor and collect important information that may someday help them predict when an earthquake will happen.

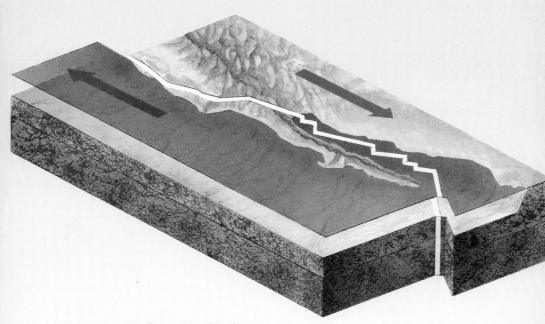

The San Andreas Fault, the source of past and future California earthquakes.

While they wait, scientists and the citizens of Parkfield are also working together, planning ways to keep people safe when an earthquake does strike. Along with town officials, disaster assistance organizations, and emergency service workers, they are hoping to save lives, homes, and businesses by being prepared.

Now Try This

Earthquakes—Be Ready!

Millions of earthquakes happen around the world every year. Earthquakes can happen anywhere, at any time.

Earthquakes cannot be prevented, and so far they cannot be reliably predicted. The best thing to do is to be prepared. Help your friends and family be prepared too!

Here is an activity for you to do with your classmates that will help keep you prepared for earthquakes.

A lightweight bag of emergency items for earthquake survival

1. Gather information about how to stay safe during an earthquake. Good sources are the American Red Cross, the Federal Emergency Management Agency (FEMA), and the USGS.

2. Contact your local government. Find out if your community has an earthquake plan or advice about how to be prepared.

3. Share your information with your family. Have a family meeting and talk about safe spots in each room of your home. Practice what to do with your family. Put together a home safety kit.

4. Help keep your friends at school safe too. Make a poster about earthquake safety for your school building. Share the poster with your class. Explain what an earthquake feels like and what to do if an earthquake hits.

Glossary

fault *n.* a break in Earth's crust.

fumes *n.* unpleasant or irritating, sometimes poisonous, gases.

instrument *n.* a special tool.

magma *n.* melted rock within Earth.

monitor *v.* to track the changes or developments of a certain situation or thing.

network *n.* a group of connected things, such as instruments, machines, or computers.

observatory *n.* a place for watching and studying happenings in nature.

prehistoric *adj.* from the time before written history.

volcanologists *n.* scientists who study volcanoes.